# A TAPESTRY

A Collection of Poems

SHYLAJA VIJAYKUMAR

Copyright © SHYLAJA VIJAYKUMAR
All Rights Reserved.

This book has been self-published with all reasonable efforts taken to make the material error-free by the author. No part of this book shall be used, reproduced in any manner whatsoever without written permission from the author, except in the case of brief quotations embodied in critical articles and reviews.

The Author of this book is solely responsible and liable for its content including but not limited to the views, representations, descriptions, statements, information, opinions, and references ["Content"]. The Content of this book shall not constitute or be construed or deemed to reflect the opinion or expression of the Publisher or Editor. Neither the Publisher nor Editor endorse or approve the Content of this book or guarantee the reliability, accuracy, or completeness of the Content published herein and do not make any representations or warranties of any kind, express or implied, including but not limited to the implied warranties of merchantability, fitness for a particular purpose.

The Publisher and Editor shall not be liable whatsoever...

Made with ❤ on the BookLeaf Publishing Platform
www.bookleafpub.in
www.bookleafpub.com

# Dedication

To my two lovely daughters - Khushi and Yasha - who have been a great support throughout.

# Preface

Writing for me is an expression of myself. Poetry is my
confidante and also a sponge which absorbs me
to such an extent that I have to search for myself in the
jumble of letters and words piled up.

# Acknowledgements

Initially, this was an attempt to unburden myself. I'm indeed very thankful to all those dear friends and family members who received the early drafts with warmth and encouragement. I'm also grateful to one of my very dear friends for his candid corrections.

This is my first collection of poems in English, a bouquet of buds I humbly offer to you, the readers, hoping that your imagination will transform the bouquet into fragrant blossoms.

# 1. Paint me if you can

Tried to paint
a picture of a girl.
The white canvas
Started to whisper.
Ignoring, I dipped the brush into the palate
Of so many colours.
Just before I could splash
The colours on to the canvas,

I heard a scream!
Followed by a voice.
Caution!
It is easy to imagine me
In all colours,
It is all so good
To win accolades
For the muted painting.
Beware of the red underneath,
The hot tear drops, disheveled hair,
Bruises all over,
The hushed voice,
Stitched lips, and vanquished breath!!

This is me.

Paint only if you can
Drape my nudity,
And splash some
Love and dignity.
I am now stuck in between
Your fingers
Paint me if you can.

# 2. The Growing Ice

White everywhere
The crunchy cold ice
"Oh snow! So cold"
Joyful screams from
The tourist crowd
Did not surprise me
Even though it was the
First visit to the snowy hills.
It was all familiar within,
The swelling pinching ice
Known for years
Will never melt in summer
Like this one that
Flows down the mountains
into the soothing lap of the
Clear blue lake.
Wearing a long coat
With a fur cap covered
To beat the cold outside
Doesn't warm up the insides
There is no lake
Which can hold the
Ice within.
Like the lush green trees

Bent down with the
Burden of the snow
I too a tourist
Pretending to be happy
Tread upon the snow
Crushing the ice
Beneath the feet.
Heaps of it grows within
Where no one visits
But me.

# 3. Castle in the Sand

From within the lapping waves
Touching the shore
The fine sprawling sand
Calls a child to build a castle
A sand castle!

The child runs in and out
Of the shore
With tiny palms of water
Creating doors and windows,
Decorates it with twigs
And pebbles.
Creativity let loose
The castle is ready!

The child runs to the busy parents to show it.
They give a snack or two and shoo the child away.
The child runs to a group of
Kids playing on the beach.
They thrust a ball into the hands and ask her to play

The child returns to the spot
But the castle is gone
Wiped out.

The forlorn child walks back to the parents.

Next evening same spot
The child is busy building a different castle
With a lot more pebbles and twigs.
After the completion
The child lies down on the sand
Head turned towards
The castle to admire what she built!!

# 4. Temple stands

Whispering prayers,
Moaning pain,
Warm tears,
Unfurling hopes,
Nude hearts at the shrine,
Surpass the art on the
Stone walls.

"Go not to the temple"
"My body the shrine"
"Do not make idols for yourselves"
The words of the seers
Drown under the ringing
Carved brass bells.

Continuous chanting,
Jostling in the long lines,
Ticketed services,
Gods campaigning
For human power
Mesmerize the atheists
And the agnostics

Shaving of heads,

Walking on the embers,
Drowning in the rivers,
Screaming calls,
Painted faces,
Bundles of crisp notes,
Gold and silver in abundance,
Do not change the static
Expression of the idols.

The temple stands,
Contextual structure ,
Churning the ideals,
Witnessing havoc and miracles ,
Breathes immortality
Into every boulder that
Grows into a carved stone
To fit in the altar.

# 5. Surface Sailing

Wings spread on the serene waters
Soaking up all the pink from the skies
Lapping up the first shimmers
From the rising sun
Hoping to anchor
Somewhere
She sails through
Dawns and dusks

Strong winds, surging waves
The scary depth of the waters
Are not seen from the bank
Seems like a swaying
Lovely gem,
A decor on the blue
Deceptive ocean.

Slowly, she anchors
Pours out the dreams and desires
On to the shore.
Stands tethered all night
Mends the tears and tatters
In the fragile sail
Which only she can detect.

Glides again with the same tenor
Just to capture another
Dawn
And reflect the pink
To the onlookers!!

# 6. Moments Matter

Middle of a meal
Or a meeting
Google pops up
Old memories without any discretion.
Oh! I looked so slim then
Did not have a single grey hair!
This was when I visited my children,
That one was just after a funeral.
Those vain moments
Of juxtaposing the past
And the present.
Feels like someone barged
Into my private home
Which I built carefully brick by brick
With windows and doors
At the right corners,
Locking up the unsafe openings.
Now with these pics
Toppling on me,
Had to expand the shrunken space
For those very old hurts
Laid heavily on my eyelids.

"Moments in the travel

Of time need to be picked
And kissed naturally"
I said this to a tech friend
"Oh! That is not a problem at all
You can actually put a cap on Google
And hide the ones you don't want to see"
Let me try this I thought
I sat at my desk with
This tiny device in my palm
Trying to filter the memories.
As I placed my finger
On the pics
I could feel a gush of many more intangible moments
Which even
Google cannot access.
I shut down the device
Opened the windows for some fresh air.
Decided to go for a walk
My tech friend waved out to me from a distance .
"Hey were you able to hide
them all", he laughed
I pulled him into the bar
Ordered a drink
And said "Come let us together
Make this moment a tangible memory"
Click! A selfie goes!

# 7. Expressions

On a rainy evening
With the  pitter patter on the window pane
I sat down to weave the letters into words
And words into lines.
Seeking the garb
To dress the thoughts
A battle ensued
Which colour, what texture?
The one I was born with?
The one I grew up with?
The ones thrust upon me.
Flailing feelings nudged
My silence
Empty page stared hard!
Letters words and lines
Gatecrashed and fell on to
White paper
Weaving their own language.
The choice was made!!

# 8. Another New year

Another new year
Is knocking on the door.
It's just another chance
To paint on the white canvas.
With the strokes anew,
To weave another tapestry
Of hopes and dreams
It's just another chance!

The whole world is celebrating,
Bursting crackers,
And singing songs.
And I am still at the
Threshold of the door
About to shut behind
All those familiar times,
Ruminating over
Just another chance!

Me and the old year
Have been buddies
Traversed together
Laughed together
Wiped each others' tears

Hoping for
Another chance together.

I hear my buddy
Knocking at the brand
New door with arms full of
God knows what gifts,
Perhaps, a colourful
Hand-post
To guide me along
The unknown paths.
I hear the knock again.
I shut the old behind
To open the new door
And greet
Just another chance!!

# 9. Born Again

A happy wrinkle,
Along with the
Already existing ones
As seen these days
Around the corner of my mouth.
Forgotten lullabies well
Out of my dry throat.
Hands curled around the
Bundle of Joy
Feels like the world
Sleeping in my arms.

Tiny eyes opening and shutting
Twisted smile on the pink lips
Wiped away all the pain
Long hidden in the caverns.
Tender fingers
Held my shaky forefinger
In a divine bond.

The shrill screams in the night
Added meaning to my
Sleepless nights.
The gurgles knocked on my

Quiet aimless mornings
And paved the way to purpose.

I am now with a new partner
To laugh and cry again ,
To hop and run around.
To make those stubborn demands,
To coin false excuses,
To fight all the battles
Old and new,
To lay down the pretentious
Heavy sack of maturity.

I just became a grandmother,
With a baby in my arms
And with a child
Prancing in my old heart.

# 10. Crossing the borders

My children live
Across the borders.
I am a mother, just a mother
Yearning to take them into
My warm folds of love.
Just when I land in that country
My heart begins to flutter
A smile appears on my parched lips
In spite of the tiring journey
My footsteps gain energy
And I float on those escalators

Oh! it's not so easy
Still so many steps before
I can really meet them.
Now I stand at the counter,
Immigration officer staring at me.
Tries to read my name.
Even though mispronounced I acknowledge!
"How long do you Intend to stay?"
"What is the purpose of your visit?"
"Don't you think u are staying a little longer?"
"How much cash have u carried?"
"Have you carried any gifts?"

With a wry smile he says
"Have you carried any curry leaves?"
His suspicious looks
Steal my privacy
I feel I am being invaded.

At last when I hug my children
I feel I have left myself
Behind those counters!

# 11. I Met My Childhood

All of a sudden
I saw her springing out
Of a heap of
Fragmented times.
Screaming with flailing arms and sprinting backwards.

Then, as if the
Winds of time stilled
She pauses
Brushes her foot
On something very familiar,
The lines of a hop scotch
I suppose.
Goes from one box to another and stands still in the
crossed box.

Am I seeing a tear
Down her cheek ?
It seemed like she
Heard some voices
And burst out laughing.

Glistening teardrops
Blended with the smile.

She beckoned to me
I walked across the
Jammed roads
And I met her!
Her eyes mirrored
The unformed rawness
Of my childhood!!
And my tears blended
With hers.

# 12. Hold my fingers

Yes baby, you can
Hold my fingers firm.
They are a bit shriveled
But these were the same
That I used, to weave life
According to my terms.

Just when I thought
Everything is over
And let loose my hands
Your tiny fingers touched
My rugged ones
Shaking me to grab life
All over again!!
Yes baby, you can
Hold my fingers firm.

Right from cupping your
Tender falling neck,
Straightening the curls,
Holding the chalk through
Those naughty slipping fingers,
Opening the wraps of your
Favourite chocolates,

Colouring my hands along with yours
Dirtying them in the mud
And washing them in the rain,
To clapping for you
On your every
Big and small doings.
These hands are
Always in yours
And I get to use them again.
This time according to your terms.
Yes baby you can
Hold my fingers firm.

# 13. Whiteness

I stood for long
And gazed at the mountains
Draped in white.
Strained my ears to hear
Lest it whispered something
Eternal silence
Surrounded me.

Strangely I could hear
Never ceasing rumbles
From within the dark crevices
Of my heart

All the whiteness outside
Failed to erase the darkness inside
And the teasing quietness
Could not melt the noise inside

Periodically visited
Snowy stubborn mountains
Simply refuse to communicate

May be it needs
Ages or may be never

Can we internalize
The language that the
Whiteness speaks !!

.

# 14. Eternal Silence

Mustard seasoning
In the kitchen
Splattered on to my face.
Autos and metro
Screeched into my ears
The piling files
On the office table
Mocked me.

I failed to hear
Tender Fluttering noises
From my womb.

Now after many years
The same fluttering noise
Speaks to me
In a language
I cannot comprehend.
I am surrounded by
Eternal Silence!!

# 15. Colours

All these leaves
Once soaked in sunshine
Are now down
On the ground.
Beautiful deep colours
Like dreams.
Treaded, blown, swept.
But still worth watching.
Seems like they will
Very soon splash
A new colour on the
Canvas of life.
Only to unravel the unknown!

# 16. To My Daughters

Little bundle of joy
Curled up in my arms
So close to my heart
Gurgles and babbles
Faltering little feet
Fingers entwined into mine
Never guessed at that time
That my love, my baby darling
Would grow into a
Charming young woman
But my heart Still
Sings lullabies
I still rock the cradle
Filled with all your
Dreams and desires
I have still preserved your
Lilting laughter and chatter
Lest you need them
I still feel your soft kicks
In my womb
Maybe you are now
Very smart.
Handling
Big trades and codes

With big people
But my baby
There is one trade
Where the deal can never
Be closed
There is one code
Which cannot
Be built
The simple coded trade of love
Between me and you.

# 17. Life Submerged

Down the steep escalators
They slide and tip toe into the crisscross of paths all laid
underground.
They set out from homes with the wings of hopes
Tethered to the fast moving tubes
Don't know what smiles are hidden underneath those
lids
Sunk into their phones.
Walking underneath the
Glass topped tunnel
Do they sense the green world
Above their heads?
First rays do not touch their hearts and their
evenings are with the neon lights .
Sudden splash of music at the end of the tunnel a
reminder of love,
Done just for alms
Is ignored by the programmed walkers.
Tied to the armed cushion chairs of the mechanized
tubes in these burrows,
Multiple destinations to harp on
Transit as well as final
Imagining all the colours out there.

Celebrate their
Submerged lives .

# 18. Picnic on the Seaside

Feels like there is
Nothing like the sea beach
But the waves also carry
The stench of death
Washed ashore!
People come on picnics
They bask under the sun
Build castles in the sand
And return to their
Brick towns
Untouched by the depth
Or the vastness of the sea!!

# 19. This Way To Love Laughter & Happily Ever After

The board read
Defining the way
To permanent joy.
Let me follow the instruction and go
In the direction marked
I thought
Nothing new encountered at the designated spot,
Humans at the finely laid tables gulping down
The chill beer
Chit chatting
Men about women
And women about men
Politics brewing
Taxes intervening
Talking properties
Lipstick smiles
Cigaretting false pride
Women in their best gowns
Men in tuxedos
Trapped in transience .
Someone known to me

Came up to me and said
"Why don't you join us?"
I looked up into his friendly eyes
Transience is the crown
Of every moment
I stood up to join
His table
I too found my way
To love laughter
And happily ever after.

# 20. Superannuation

Over, they said all of a sudden
Pushed every little thing
Behind the curtains.
Discarding the role,
Wiping the painted face,
Walked out of the settings
Into the audience free
Open arena.
And the fearless cool breeze
Brushed against my heart.
Fragrance of the fast withering
Garlands around my neck
Filled the caverns of my mind.
Hidden amidst the band wagon
Of all those memories
My name sans designations
Sparkled my identity

One more stage
One other play
Yet another role
Got ready to enact
But this time
Just for my sake

# 21. Fog

A light blue silky veil
Descended on the
Buzzing activity and
Buried life into nothingness.
Suspended all the dreams,
Wrapped up the world
In its blanket with no hole
To peep through!

Suddenly, the shroud lifted
The stubborn city reappeared
With hope surging
Amidst the vast expanse
Of impenetrable blue!!

www.ingramcontent.com/pod-product-compliance
Lightning Source LLC
LaVergne TN
LVHW041243200726
843507LV00013B/2800

www.ingramcontent.com/pod-product-compliance
Lightning Source LLC
LaVergne TN
LVHW041247200726
843507LV00013B/2856